W9-AZA-181

LEARNING MANUAL FOR
How the Brain Learns

Dr. David A. Sousa

CORWIN PRESS, INC.
A Sage Publications Company
Thousand Oaks, California

Copyright © 1998 by David A. Sousa

All rights reserved. No part of this book may be reproduced or utilized in any form or by any means, electronic or mechanical, including photocopying, recording, or by any information storage and retrieval system, without permission in writing from the publisher.

For information address:

Corwin Press, Inc.
A Sage Publications Company
2455 Teller Road
Thousand Oaks, California 91320
E-mail: order@corwinpress.com

SAGE Publications Ltd.
6 Bonhill Street
London EC2A 4PU
United Kingdom

SAGE Publications India Pvt. Ltd.
M-32 Market
Greater Kailash I
New Delhi 110 048 India

Printed in the United States of America

ISBN 0-8039-6753-5

This book is printed on acid-free paper.

98 99 00 01 02 03   10 9 8 7 6 5 4 3 2

Production Editor: S. Marlene Head

Table of Contents

About the Author

David A. Sousa is an international educational consultant, a former chemistry teacher and school superintendent, and author of the popular book *How the Brain Learns* (published by the National Association of Secondary School Principals). He has a bachelor's degree in chemistry from Massachusetts State College at Bridgewater, a master's degree in teaching science from Harvard University, and a doctorate from Rutgers University.

He has conducted hundreds of workshops in instructional skills, brain research, and science education at the elementary, secondary, and university levels, and at national conventions of educational organizations. He has served as an adjunct professor at Seton Hall and Rutgers Universities. Sousa has published dozens of articles in leading journals. He was president of the National Staff Development Council in 1992 and was a 1996 recipient of the W. K. Kellogg Foundation Expert-in-Residence Grant. In 1997, he was part of an international team that worked in the Ukraine with master teachers from the former Soviet Republics.

Introduction

This manual is designed to accompany the author's book, *How the Brain Learns,* published in 1995 by the National Association of Secondary School Principals (NASSP). It contains an update on research information that has come forth since the book was published. Also included are activities that will help readers understand and practice some of the ideas presented in the book, as well as devise strategies that are appropriate for their own circumstances.

In the past few years, more educators have become interested in brain research and its potential applications to educational practice. Signs of this increased awareness are everywhere. Staff development programs are devoting more time to this area, more books about the brain are available, brain-compatible teaching units are sprouting up, and the journals of most major educational organizations have devoted special issues to the topic.

Although research continues to provide a deeper understanding of the workings of the human brain, educators need to be cautious about how they apply these findings to practice. There is, of course, no panacea that will make teaching and learning a perfect process — and that includes brain research. It *is* a long leap from making a research finding to changing schools and practice *because* of that finding. What I have tried to do here is report on research (from both the behavioral and cognitive sciences) that seems to be sufficiently reliable that it can enhance our practice. These are exciting times for educators, but we must ensure that we don't let the excitement cloud our common sense.

The author is particularly interested in receiving comments and suggestions from educators and others who have read *How the Brain Learns* and who have used this manual. Comments can be sent to:

Dr. David A. Sousa
P.O. Box 136
Fanwood, NJ 07023

Note: The pages referred to in parentheses in each activity are those found in *How the Brain Learns*, and the abbreviation *HBL* is used in certain places as a reminder.

Dear Diary,

Please allow every teacher to realize the awesome power they hold in their hands, and that they are the doors through which whole new worlds of possibility can open for their students. That by understanding students, day to day, and not judging them or shutting out the many opportunities for their success, teachers can, and often do, make all the difference.

Sandi Redenbach, *Autobiography of a Dropout: Dear Diary*
(Reprinted with permission)

Chapter 1 - Basic Brain Facts

Key Points to Ponder

Jot down on this page key points, ideas, strategies, and resources you want to consider later. This sheet is your personal journal summary and will help to jog your memory.

_____

_____

_____

_____

_____

_____

_____

_____

_____

_____

_____

_____

_____

Research Update

Is the "Novel" Brain What Makes Today's Students Different?

We often hear teachers remark that students are more different today in the way they learn than ever before. They seem to have a shorter attention span and bore easily. Why is that? Is there something happening in the environment of learners that alters the way they approach the learning process? Here is a likely explanation.

From the moment of birth (some say earlier), the brain is collecting information and learning from its environment. The home environment of a child several decades ago was usually quiet — some might say boring. Parents and children did a lot of talking and reading. The occasional radio program was an exciting event. For these children, school was a much more interesting place because it had television, films, field trips, and guest speakers — experiences not usually found at home. Because there were few other distractions, school was an important influence in a child's life.

In recent years, children have been growing up in a very different environment. The rapidly changing multimedia-based culture and the stresses from an ever-increasing pace of living are changing what the developing brain learns from the world. Children have become accustomed to these rapid sensory and emotional changes and respond by engaging in all types of activities of short duration at home and in the malls. By acclimating itself to these changes, the brain responds more readily to the unique and different — what I now call "novelty." Adult skeptics need but watch MTV for just a few minutes to discover that the images change every few seconds and play heavily on emotions.

School is but one of many factors influencing today's children. They are wrestling with the need to be different while under pressure to conform. They have to develop and deal with relationships, identify peer groups, and respond to religious influences. Add to this mix the changes in family patterns and lifestyles, as well as the effects of diet, drugs, and sleep deprivation, and we can realize how very different the environment of today's child is from that of just 15 years ago.

Schools and teaching, however, haven't changed much. In many schools, the computers provide few of the options that students get with their more powerful computers at home. In high schools, lecturing continues to be the main method of instruction, and the overhead projector is often the most advanced technology used. Students remark that school is a dull, nonengaging environment that is much less interesting than what is available outside school. They have a difficult time focusing for extended periods and are easily distracted. Because they see little novelty and relevancy in what they are learning, they keep asking the eternal question, "Why do we need to know this?"

Educators can either decry the changing brain and culture or recognize that we must adjust schools to accommodate these changes. Now that we have a more scientifically based understanding about today's "novel" brain and how it learns, we must rethink what we do in classrooms and schools.

The "Windows of Opportunity" Research

This research examines how the young brain grows and learns. A newborn's brain makes connections at an incredible pace as the child absorbs its environment. The richer the environment, the greater the number of interconnections that are made, and learning takes place faster and with greater meaning. As the child grows, connections that the brain finds useful become permanent, and those not useful are eliminated. The brain is selectively strengthening and pruning connections based on experience. This process continues throughout our lives but seems to be most pronounced between the ages of 2 and 11, as windows in different development areas open and close.

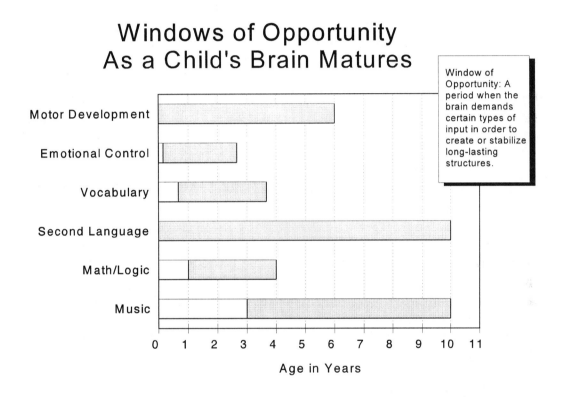

These windows represent critical periods when the brain demands certain types of input to create or consolidate neural networks. The window for developing emotional control, for example, seems to be from 2 to 30 months. Certainly, one can learn to control emotions after that age. But what the child learned *during* that window period will be difficult to change and will strongly influence what is learned after the window closes. The window for acquiring a second language with the same fluency as the child's native tongue closes around the age of 10 or 11.

This research suggests that an enriched home and preschool environment, especially during the early years, can help children build neural connections and make full use of their mental abilities.

Learning How We Read: Does Research Support Phonics or Whole Language?

The most recent research into how the brain reads may finally bring an end to the decades-old debate over whether phonics or whole language is the better way to teach reading. This research is revealing that the brain reads by breaking works into sounds. Using MRI technology, Drs. Sally and Bennett Shaywitz at Yale University measured the flow of blood to brain cells. They discovered that people who know how to sound out words have a rapid increase in blood supply to the brain's language centers and can rapidly process what they see. Conversely, people who can't sound out words have a decreased blood supply to these language centers. Thus, *without the ability to sound out words, the brain is baffled*! There is no explanation now as to the cause of the decreased blood flow. However, researchers have found that the reading abilities of these students improved dramatically when they were given intensive training in sound-letter awareness in kindergarten and first grade.

These findings support those documented over the past 20 years by the National Institutes of Health (NIH): Children need to understand the sounds of the language and sound-letter relationships (phonics) before they can learn to read. This ability comes naturally to some students; others need to be taught. The NIH studies also found that at least 95% of even the poorest readers can learn to read at grade level if they are given early and proper instruction in sound-letter relationships, followed by exposure to literature.

The research done at Yale and by NIH strongly suggests that we must abandon the notion that phonics and whole language are competing and mutually exclusive approaches to teaching reading. *Both are needed!* Children learn to read best when first trained in recognizing phonemes and then taught sound-letter relationships, blending and sounding out words (phonics method). Simultaneously, teachers should present literature to children by reading to them and offering interesting books for them to read (whole language method).

Activity 1.1 - Fist for a Brain (HBL, p. 2)

This activity shows how you can use your fists to represent the human brain.

1. Extend both arms with palms open and facing down.

2. Lock your thumbs.

3. Curl your fingers to make two fists.

4. Turn your fists inward until the knuckles touch.

5. While the fists are touching, pull both toward your chest until you are looking down on your knuckles. This is the approximate size of your brain! The thumbs are the front and are crossed to remind us that the left side of the brain controls the right side of the body, and the right side of the brain controls the left side of the body. The knuckles and outside part of the hands represent the **cerebrum** or thinking part of the brain.

6. Spread your palms apart while keeping the knuckles touching. Look at the tips of your fingers, which represent the **limbic** or emotional system. Note how this system is buried deep within the brain.

7. The wrists are the **brainstem** where vital body functions (such as body temperature, heart beat, blood pressure) are controlled. Rotating your hands shows how the brain can move on top of the spinal column, which is represented by your forearms.

Activity 1.2 - Review of Brain Area Functions (HBL, p. 4)

Write below your *own* key words and phrases to describe the functions of each of the five brain areas. Then write each brain area in the diagram below on the appropriate arrow stem.

Cerebrum: _____

_____

Hippocampus: _____

_____

Amygdala: _____

_____

Cerebellum: _____

_____

Brain stem: _____

_____

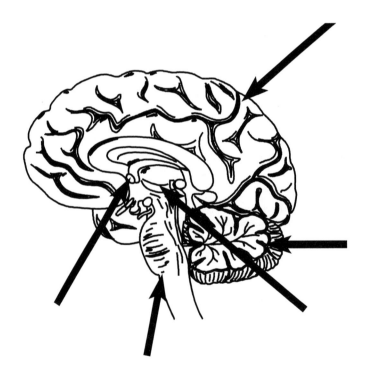

How would you describe the difference between the mind and the brain?

_____

_____

_____

_____

Chapter 2 - How the Brain Processes Information

Key Points to Ponder

 Jot down on this page key points, ideas, strategies, and resources you want to consider later. This sheet is your personal journal summary and will help to jog your memory.

_____

_____

_____

_____

_____

_____

_____

_____

_____

_____

_____

Research Update

Sensory Engagement During Learning

The cognitive research reaffirms strongly that we learn best when we are actively involved in interesting and challenging situations, and when we *talk* about the learning. Task-centered talking is critical to the memory process because it helps maintain focus while enhancing sense and meaning. Yet, in too many schools students sit quietly and passively for long stretches in rooms with little visual stimulation, listening primarily to teachers talk.

Districts must provide the technology and materials needed to make schools engaging and interesting. Teachers need to use a multisensory approach consistently so that students are actively involved in their learning. Classrooms should be visually appealing places where learners are teachers and teachers are learners. At appropriate intervals, students should be standing up, moving about (there's 15% more blood in the brain when we stand), and discussing with each other what they are learning *while* learning it. This social interaction is also emotionally stimulating and enhances the learning process.

Understanding Emotions in Learning (HBL, p. 13)

Daniel Goleman's 1995 book, *Emotional Intelligence*, summarized the breakthroughs in understanding the strong influence that emotions have as we grow and learn. How a person "feels" about a learning situation determines the amount of attention devoted to it. Emotions interact with reason to support or inhibit learning. To be successful learners and productive citizens, we need to know how to use our emotions intelligently.

Over the years, most teacher-training classes have told prospective teachers to focus on reason and avoid emotions in their lessons. Now we need to enlighten educators about how emotions consistently affect attention and learning. For example, students must feel physically safe and emotionally secure in their schools and classrooms before they can process the enormous amount of information we give them. Districts must ensure, therefore, that schools are free of weapons and violence. Teachers can then promote emotional security by establishing a positive climate that encourages students to take risks. Students must sense that the teacher wants to help them be right rather than catch them being wrong.

Moreover, superintendents and board members need to examine their actions, which set the emotional climate of a district. Is it a place where people want to come to work? Does the district reward or frown on appropriate risk taking?

We also have to explore what and how we teach students about their emotions. Goleman suggests we teach about such topics as controlling impulses, delaying gratification, expressing feelings, managing relationships, and reducing stress. Students should recognize that they can manage their emotions for greater productivity and can develop emotional skills for greater success in life.

Enhance Meaning by Making Connections to Past Experiences (HBL, p. 17)

Past experiences always influence new learning. What we already know acts as a filter, helping us attend to those things that have meaning (i.e., relevancy) and discard those that don't. Meaning, therefore, has a great impact on whether information and skills will be learned and stored. If students have not found meaning by the end of a learning episode, there is little likelihood that much will be remembered.

Teachers spend nearly 90% of their planning time devising lessons so that students will *understand* the learning objective (i.e., make *sense* of it). But to convince a learner's brain to persist with that objective, teachers need to work harder at helping students establish *meaning*. We should remember that what was meaningful for *us* as children may not be necessarily meaningful for children today.

If we expect students to find meaning, we need to be certain that today's curriculum contains connections to *their* past experiences, not just ours. Further, the size and the strict separation of the secondary curriculum areas do little to help students find the time to make relevant connections between and among subjects. Helping students to make connections between subject areas by integrating the curriculum increases meaning and retention, especially when students recognize a future use for the new learning.

Meaning is so powerful that most states prohibit trial lawyers from using what is dubbed the "golden rule" argument. It asks the jury, "If you were in this person's situation, what would you have done?"

Activity 2.1 - Walking Through the Brain (HBL, p. 11)

(**Note:** In the model diagram on page 11 [*HBL*], the lines representing the perceptual register were inadvertently omitted in earlier printings of the book. They are a series of slanted lines, drawn vertically, that are the metaphor of venetian blinds and should be drawn between the column of arrows and the clipboard.)

Directions: In this activity, we will assume the roles of the different parts of the brain processing model.

1. Each participant gets one of the following assignments:

> 3-4 persons for the **perceptual register**
> 1 person for the **short-term memory**
> 1 person for the **working memory**
> 3-4 persons for the **long-term storage**
> rest of the class represents **incoming information**

2. In an open area of the classroom, the participants should arrange themselves in a pattern that approximates the model on page 11 of *HBL*.

3. All participants, except those representing **incoming information**, briefly explain their role and function in the model.

4. The participants representing **incoming information** then move through the model one at a time, explaining what is happening at each stage.

5. **Variations:** Replay the activity demonstrating how information can be accepted or rejected by the perceptual register, short-term memory, and working memory. One of the participants representing **long-term storage** can also represent the feedback loop of past experiences.

6. After demonstrating several different possibilities, discuss in groups of two how this activity may have enhanced your understanding of the model. Note the effect that kinesthetic activity can have on learning new material.

Activity 2.2 - Redesigning the Information Processing Model (HBL, p. 11)

Directions: Working in groups of three, redesign on chart paper the information processing model on page 11 using different metaphors for each of the major parts of the model. When finished, post the chart paper on the wall and be prepared to explain the metaphors and why you chose them.

If you like, you can use the space below to sketch out the model before transferring it to the chart paper.

Activity 2.3 - Threats and Emotions in School (HBL, pp. 13-14)

 Working with your partner, use webs or other graphic organizers (see *HBL*, pages 100-107, for examples of organizers) to map out your responses to each of the following questions (A-D).

A. What kinds of emotions in school could interfere with cognitive processing (i.e., have a negative effect on learning)?

(Draw your organizer here)

B. What strategies and structures can schools and teachers use to limit the threat and negative effects of these emotions?

(Draw your organizer here)

Activity 2.3 Continued

C. What factors in schools can foster emotions in students that promote learning (i.e., have a positive effect)?

(Draw your organizer here)

D. What strategies have you used to encourage the positive emotions that promote learning?

(Draw your organizer here)

Summary: Based on your input in questions A-D, what role does the affect (emotions) play in cognitive processing?

_____

_____

_____

_____

Activity 2.4 - Sense and Meaning (HBL, pp. 16-18)

??? ???

Discuss with a partner some examples of learnings that (for most students) . . .

A. Make *sense* but have little or no meaning

_____

_____

_____

_____

B. Have *meaning* but make little or no sense

_____

_____

_____

_____

How could you add the sense or meaning missing in the examples above?

_____

_____

_____

_____

Activity 2.5 - The Modality Preferences Instrument (HBL, p. 23)

Follow the directions below to get a score that will indicate your own modality (sense) preference(s). This instrument is just one of many available, and you should not rely on just one instrument for self-assessment. Keep in mind that sensory preferences are usually evident only during prolonged and complex learning tasks.

Identifying Sensory Preferences

Directions: For each item, circle "A" if you **agree** that the statement describes you most of the time. Circle "D" if you **disagree** that the statement describes you most of the time.

1.	I prefer reading a story rather than listening to someone tell it.	A	D
2.	I would rather watch television than listen to the radio.	A	D
3.	I remember names better than faces.	A	D
4.	I like classrooms with lots of posters and pictures around the room.	A	D
5.	The appearance of my handwriting is important to me.	A	D
6.	I think more often in pictures.	A	D
7.	I am distracted by visual disorder or movement.	A	D
8.	I have difficulty remembering directions that were told to me.	A	D
9.	I would rather watch athletic events than participate in them.	A	D
10.	I tend to organize my thoughts by writing them down.	A	D
11.	My facial expression is a good indicator of my emotions.	A	D
12.	I tend to remember names better than faces.	A	D
13.	I would enjoy taking part in dramatic events like plays.	A	D
14.	I tend to subvocalize and think in sounds.	A	D
15.	I am easily distracted by sounds.	A	D
16.	I easily forget what I read unless I talk about it.	A	D
17.	I would rather listen to the radio than watch television.	A	D
18.	My handwriting is not very good.	A	D
19.	When faced with a problem, I tend to talk it through.	A	D
20.	I express my emotions verbally.	A	D
21.	I would rather be in a group discussion than read about a topic.	A	D

22. I prefer talking on the phone rather than writing a letter to someone.   A   D

23. I would rather participate in athletic events than watch them.   A   D

24. I prefer going to museums where I can touch the exhibits.   A   D

25. My handwriting deteriorates when the space becomes smaller   A   D

26. My mental pictures are usually accompanied by movement.   A   D

27. I like being outdoors and doing things like biking, camping, swimming, hiking, etc.   A   D

28. I remember best what was done rather what was seen or talked about.   A   D

29. When faced with a problem, I often select the solution involving the greatest activity.   A   D

30. I like to make models or other hand-crafted items.   A   D

31. I would rather do experiments rather than read about them.   A   D

32. My body language is a good indicator of my emotions.   A   D

33. I have difficulty remembering verbal directions if I have not done the activity before.   A   D

Interpreting the Instrument's Score

Total the number of "**A**" responses in items 1-11:   _____
This is your visual score.

Total the number of "**A**" responses in items 12-22:   _____
This is your auditory score.

Total the number of "**A**" responses in items 23-33:   _____
This is your tactile/kinesthetic score.

If you scored a lot higher in any one area: This indicates that this modality is *very probably* your preference during a protracted and complex learning situation.

If you scored a lot lower in any one area: This indicates that this modality is *not likely* to be your preference(s) in a learning situation.

If you got similar scores in all three areas: This indicates that you can learn things in almost any way they are presented.

Activity 2.5 Continued

Questions About Your Results:

A. What was your preferred modality? Were you surprised?

_____

_____

B. How does this preference show up in your daily life?

_____

_____

_____

C. How does this preference show up in your teaching?

_____

_____

_____

D. Discuss A through C above with a partner.

Activity 2.6 - Increasing Processing Time Through Motivation (HBL, p. 26)

This **Practitioner's Corner** on p. 26 of *HBL* discusses one of the variables of motivation called the *level of concern*. If we have no concern about a particular learning, then there is little chance we will learn it. On the other hand, when we recognize a need to acquire information or a skill, moderate stress or concern results, and that emotion is more likely to lead to learning.

The figure below shows that as the level of concern increases, so does the degree of learning. Of course, if the stress level gets too high, "downshifting" occurs, we go past the optimum level, and we shift our focus to the emotions generated by the stress and learning fades.

Read the **Practitioner's Corner** to determine the four factors that raise or lower the level of concern, and then answer questions A and B below.

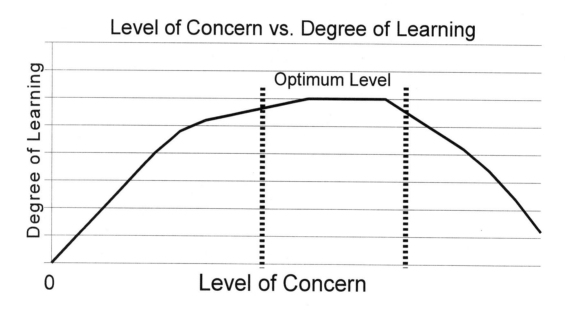

A. What are some class activities that increase the level of concern beyond the optimum level?

_____

_____

_____

_____

Activity 2.6 Continued

B. What strategies lower the level of concern raised by the activities in your answers to A above?

_____

_____

_____

_____

_____

_____

Summary: Discuss in groups of three the various activities you put down in A and B above.

Activity 2.7 - Testing Whether Information Is in Long-Term Storage (HBL, pp. 29-30)

Directions: Read pages 29 and 30 (*HBL*).

A. Summarize here the ***implications*** of what you have read for learning and testing.

_____

_____

_____

_____

_____

_____

B. How will the above affect what you do in the classroom? Jot down some of your ideas here.

_____

_____

_____

_____

_____

_____

C. Discuss with a partner what you wrote in A and B above.

Activity 2.8 - Neurobingo

In this activity the entire class gets up and moves around. Each person tries to find someone who can answer one of the questions in a box. The person who answers the question initials the box. The object is to get a bingo pattern (horizontally, vertically, or diagonally). No person may initial the same sheet twice. Time limit: 15-20 minutes depending on the size of the group.

Find a person who is able to

Explain the function of the perceptual register	Explain the importance of sense and meaning to learning	Define "Windows of Opportunity"	Explain how the brain prioritizes incoming information	Name the sensory modalities
State the two functions of the hippocampus	Tell you the function of short-term memory	Explain the function of the amygdala	Explain what is meant by the "novel" brain	Provide an example of how self-concept affects learning
Relate the cognitive belief system to learning	Tell you the function of the cerebellum	Tell you the function of the cerebrum	Describe the time limits of working memory	Explain synapses
Explain the three cognitive spurts	Describe the capacity limits of working memory	Explain what is meant by emotional control	Explain the function of neuro-transmitters	Explain the function of long-term memory
Explain the value of humor in learning	Explain chunking	Describe the sources of brain research	Explain the importance of adequate sleep for learning	Describe a neuron

PRACTITIONER'S CORNER

Using Synergy to Enhance Learning

This strategy gets students moving and talking *while* learning. It is effective because it is multimodality, uses active participation, is emotionally stimulating, and encourages socialization. Each participant ends up having a better understanding as a result of this interaction (synergy). It can be used from the primary grades to graduate school.

- **Time for Reflection.** After teaching a concept, ask students to quietly review their notes and be prepared to explain what they have learned to someone else. Be sure to allow sufficient time for this mental rehearsal to occur.

- **Stand, Move, and Deliver.** Ask the students to walk across the room and pair up with someone they don't usually work with or know very well. They stand face-to-face and take turns explaining what they have learned. They are to add to their notes anything their partners have said that they don't have. When they are through, all students end up with more information and ideas than they would have had if they worked alone. If they cannot agree or don't understand something, they are to ask about it when the activity is over. (Note: Make sure students are standing face-to-face — rather than just looking at each other's notes — so that they must talk to their partner. Allow pairs only — one trio, if you have an odd number of students.)

- **Keep in Motion.** Move around the room using proximity to help students stay on task. Answer questions to get them back on track, but avoid reteaching the lesson. Otherwise, students will become dependent on your reteaching rather than on each other's explanations.

- **Provide and Adjust the Time.** Be sure to allow adequate time for this process to be effective. Start with a few minutes, adding more time if they are still on task and reducing the time when you sense they are done.

- **Accountability.** To help keep students on task, tell them that you will call on several students at random when the activity is over to explain what they discussed.

- **Clarify Any Misunderstandings.** Ask if there were any misunderstandings or items that need further explanation, and clarify them.

- **Use Variety for the Pairing.** Use a variety of techniques for the pairing. Aim for random pairing as much as practicable to enhance socialization and avoid monotony.

Chapter 3 - Memory, Retention, and Learning

Key Points to Ponder

Jot down on this page key points, ideas, strategies, and resources you want to consider later. This sheet is your personal journal summary and will help to jog your memory.

_____

_____

_____

_____

_____

_____

_____

_____

_____

_____

_____

Research Update

Shorter Is Better (HBL Manual, pp. 2, 30-33)

Because today's students are accustomed to quick change and novelty in their environment, many find it difficult to concentrate on the same topic for long periods of time. They fidget, drift, or get into off-task conversations. This is particularly true if the teacher is doing most of the work, such as lecturing. Timing in the lesson *is* crucial. Remember the primacy-recency effect: We tend to remember best that which comes first in a learning segment, and remember second best that which comes last. Moreover, the percentage of remembering time increases as the learning episode shortens, and it decreases as the lesson time lengthens.

This effect has a particularly important impact in block scheduling, where an 80-minute period can be a blessing or a disaster, depending on how the time is used. A block containing four 20-minute segments will often be much more productive than one continuous lesson.

Further, only one or two of the four block segments should be teacher directed. Here are some kinds of activities that can be carried out during the remaining segments.

Examples of Block Lesson Activities:

> Teacher talk (maximum of 2 segments of 10 to 15 minutes each)
> Research
> Cooperative learning groups
> Reading
> Peer coaching
> Labs (computer/application)
> Journal writing
> Guest speakers
> Videos/movies/slides
> Reflection time
> Discussion groups
> Role-playing/simulations
> Instructional games/puzzles

Rest Between Segments

Although most teachers believe that staying on task throughout the learning period is best, the research seems to indicate that neurons need some downtime to consolidate information. Coupling this with the "novelty effect" discussed earlier suggests that we are more likely to keep students focused *during* the lesson segments if we go off task *between* the segments. Here's how that might look graphically.

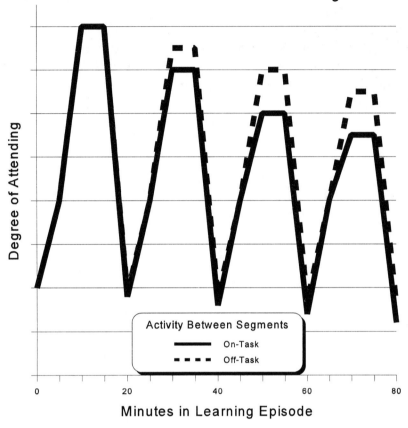

Comparison of Degree of Attending Using On-Task or Off-Task Activities Between Segments

Y-axis: Degree of Attending

X-axis: Minutes in Learning Episode (0, 20, 40, 60, 80)

Activity Between Segments
— On-Task
- - - Off-Task

The Changing Biological Rhythms

Our daily biological rhythms vary with age. The figure on page 26 shows the comparison between the typical adult and adolescent cognitive cycles during the day. Note that the adolescent cycle is shifted about an hour later. The rhythms responsible for overall intellectual performance start later in the day for an adolescent than for an adult. Because of this shift in rhythms, teenagers are sleepier in the morning and tend to stay up later at night. They also tend to perform better in problem-solving and memory tasks later in the day rather than earlier.

We need to look at what and when in the school day we ask students to perform certain tasks, such as taking tests. District leaders may want to consider realigning opening times and course schedules more closely with the students' biological rhythms to increase the chances of successful learning. Some school districts, such as Minnetonka, Minnesota, are now experimenting with later starting times for their high schools.

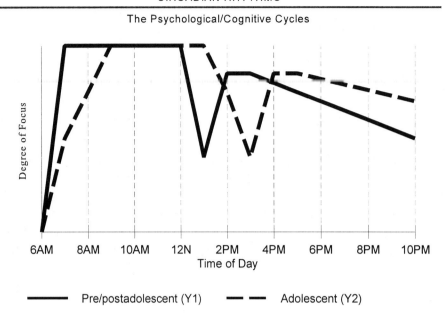

CIRCADIAN RHYTHMS

The Psychological/Cognitive Cycles

Degree of Focus

6AM   8AM   10AM   12N   2PM   4PM   6PM   8PM   10PM
Time of Day

——— Pre/postadolescent (Y1)   — — Adolescent (Y2)

The Brown University Sleep Research Laboratory has also conducted studies recently on adolescent sleep habits. They have shown that inadequate sleep results in student sleepiness earlier in the day, which limits their motivation to learn and affects their academic performance. In contrast, these students go to after-school jobs when they are more alert and more productive. Thus, sleep deprivation and circadian shifts may lead to disaffection with school and a preference for the after-school jobs.

The Importance of Sleep in Learning and Memory

The encoding of information into the long-term memory sites likely occurs during sleep, more specifically, during the rapid-eye movement (REM) stage. This is a slow process and can flow easier when the brain is not preoccupied with external stimuli. What we think and talk about while awake very likely influences the nature and shape of the memory consolidation that occurs during sleep.

Adequate sleep is vital to the memory storage process, especially for young learners. Most teenagers need about 9 hours of sleep each night. Many teenagers are not getting enough sleep. There are several factors responsible for eroding sleep time. In the morning, high schools start earlier, teens spend more time grooming, and some travel long distances to school. At the end of the day, there are athletic and social events, part-time jobs, and homework. Add to this the shift in their body clocks that tends to keep them up later (see above), and the average sleep time is more like 5 to 6 hours.

This sleep deprivation not only disturbs the memory storage process but can lead to other problems as well. Students may nod off in class, become irritable, or worse, their decreased alertness due to fatigue can lead to accidents. It is important to remind students of the importance of sleep to their mental and physical health and to encourage them to reexamine their daily activities to provide for adequate sleep.

Avoid Practicing Different Skills Too Close Together (HBL, p. 45)

Researchers at Johns Hopkins University recently found that it takes roughly 6 hours for a new skill to be consolidated and tagged for long-term storage. This reorganizing takes place while the person is off task, taking a leisurely stroll or sorting laundry. This may also explain why downtime is a good time for learners to process what they have just learned.

The researchers further discovered that those who attempted to learn a second task before the first one was fully processed had trouble doing either one well. Apparently, the presence of the first skill in working memory makes it harder to learn the second one, whereas the second skill dilutes the memory of the first. Keep in mind, too, that the more similar the second skill is to the first, the greater the likelihood of confusion. For example, one should avoid trying to learn within a short time frame how to swing a baseball bat, and then how to swing a golf club. This research is reminding us that practice makes permanent. It is better to practice one skill and learn it well *before* trying to learn (or teach) another one.

Cramming (HBL, p. 51)

The reason cramming does not result in long-term storage can be explained by the chemistry of memory. Nerve signals activate certain proteins which strengthen the nerve connections that form a memory (engram). This process requires sufficient time for the activating proteins to recycle and further strengthen the memory. In cramming, there is usually not enough time for the activating proteins to recycle, thereby reducing the probability of long-term storage.

Activity 3.1 - Rehearsal (HBL, pp. 35-36 and 55-57)

There are two types of rehearsal, and each type serves a different purpose.

Rote: Deliberate, continuous repetition of material in the same form it entered working memory (examples: telephone numbers, alphabetical order, a poem)

List below some topics you teach that should be processed and remembered through rote rehearsal:

_____

_____

_____

_____

_____

_____

_____

_____

_____

_____

_____

_____

Activity 3.1 Continued

Elaborative: Integrating information to give it sense and meaning and to create chunks (examples: compare and contrast two wars or plays; explain similarities and differences among organisms; critique a painting or musical piece)

List below some topics you teach that should be processed and remembered through elaborative rehearsal:

_____

_____

_____

_____

_____

_____

_____

_____

_____

_____

Summary: Studies show us that almost 80% of rehearsal time in schools (especially high schools) is **rote rehearsal**. Discuss in a group of three *why* this is so and what *implications* it has for learning.

Activity 3.2 - The Primacy-Recency Effect (HBL, pp. 37-43 and 58)

Directions: Read pages 37-43 and 58 in *HBL*. Then study the chart below. It illustrates the primacy-recency effect.

The effect begins as soon as the brain focuses on the learning situation. Therefore, not only what but *when* the teacher presents information or a skill can be a major factor in determining how much students remember. *Timing*, therefore, is very important.

Primacy-Recency Effect

Prime-time-1	Learn BEST — The FIRST
Down-Time	Learn LEAST — Just Past the Middle
Prime-time-2	Learn NEXT Best — The LAST

Activity 3.2 Continued

The Primacy-Recency Effect in the Classroom

Below is a sketch of two lessons. One is taught by Mr. Blue and the other by Mr. Green. Study their lesson sequences and then answer the questions below.

Mr. Blue	Lesson Sequence	Mr. Green
"Get ready to tell me the two causes of the Civil War we discussed yesterday." After getting this he then says, "Today we will learn the third and most important cause as we are still living with its aftereffects 130 years later." "Before I tell you, let me give back some homework, collect today's homework, collect the notes from Bill and Mary who were absent yesterday, take attendance, and read a brief announcement."	**Prime-time-1**	"Get ready to tell me the two causes of World War I we discussed yesterday." After getting this he then says, "Today we will learn the third and most important cause as it set the stage for another world war just 30 years later." "And here is the third cause!" (Presents third cause, gives examples, and relates it to yesterday's two causes.)
"Here is the third cause." (Presents third cause, gives examples, and relates it to yesterday's two causes.)	**Down-time**	"Go into your discussion groups and discuss this third cause. Not only tie it to the two causes we learned yesterday, but also to other wars we have learned so far. What are the similarities and differences?"
"OK, I see we've got only 5 minutes to the end of the period. You've listened attentively so you can do anything you want as long as you are quiet."	**Prime-time-2**	"Take 2 minutes to review quietly to yourself what you learned about this third cause. Be prepared to share your thoughts with the class."

Activity 3.2 Continued

With a partner, discuss the lesson sequences of Mr. Blue and Mr. Green. If these sequences are representative of what happens most of the time in their classes, whose students are more likely to remember what they have learned over time? Why?

Jot down below the *implications* of what you discussed.

_____

_____

_____

_____

_____

_____

_____

_____

_____

_____

_____

_____

Activity 3.2 Continued

The next figure shows how the proportion of prime times to downtime changes with the length of the learning episode. (Refer to the table on page 42 of *HBL.*) This information is particularly important for teachers to know who are or will be involved with block scheduling. Simply doing the same activity for a longer period of time could lead to a large chunk of downtime rather than effective learning during the prime times.

Approximate Ratio of Prime Times to Downtime During Learning Episode

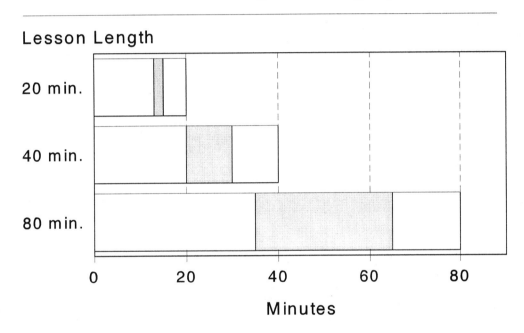

Average Prime and Downtimes in a Learning Episode			
Episode Time	Prime-Time-1	Downtime	Prime-Time-2
20 minutes	10	2	8
40 minutes	20	10	10
80 minutes	25	30	25

Summary: In groups of three, discuss how you would organize your lessons based on what you know about the primacy-recency effect.

Activity 3.3 - Definitions of Intelligence (HBL, p. 47)

Read the paragraph on page 47 (*HBL*) that gives a working definition of intelligence. Intelligence is defined here as the "rate of learning." There are, of course, other current definitions of intelligence, but they all accept the notion that intelligence is a multifaceted rather than a single entity.

Here are some other definitions:

Howard Gardner (of Harvard, who developed the notion of multiple intelligences): Intelligence is an individual's ability to use a skill, create products, or solve problems in a way that is valued by the society of that individual.

Robert Sternberg (of Yale): Intelligence is the ability to know your own strengths and weaknesses and to capitalize on the strengths while compensating for the weaknesses.

How do these modern notions of intelligence compare with your own understanding of intelligence? Write in the box below what impact these various definitions of intelligence may or may not have on how you teach.

Pick two or three of your points to share in a group of three.

_____

_____

_____

_____

_____

_____

Activity 3.4 - Chunking (HBL, pp. 49-51, 62-63)

CHUNKING

Chunking: The grouping of any coherent items of information so that we can remember them as easily as a single item.

Think of a major concept that you have taught (or presented) recently. Identify the components (sublearnings) of that concept. Chart or diagram below how you could link together the components of that concept into fewer chunks.

Activity 3.5 - Mnemonics (HBL, pp. 64-65)

 The word *mnemonics* comes from the Greek word that means "to remember." It can be a very valuable memory device, particularly with right-hemisphere-dominant learners who need a picture or other type of pattern or scheme to remember seemingly unrelated items. Mnemonics are examples of *chunking* that rely on words or the alphabet to create artificial meaning.

A. In groups of three, list here any mnemonics that you now use in the classroom. Be prepared to share at least one of the group's mnemonics with the entire class.

_____

_____

_____

_____

_____

B. Develop here other mnemonics that would help your students remember information.

_____

_____

_____

_____

_____

_____

_____

Chapter 4 - The Power of Transfer

Key Points to Ponder

Jot down on this page key points, ideas, strategies, and resources you want to consider later. This sheet is your personal journal summary and will help to jog your memory.

_____

_____

_____

_____

_____

_____

_____

_____

_____

_____

_____

_____

Research Update

Emotions and Transfer

Past experiences always affect new learning. Studies (see Bower, 1992; Goleman, 1995) show that a person's emotional state greatly influences what they recall during a learning episode. Feelings of sadness or ineptness make it easier to recall unpleasant experiences, like rejection or failure. This recall of negative past experiences can unwittingly intensify the sad feeling and ultimately lead to depression.

Happy feelings, on the other hand, make it easier to recall positive experiences, like acceptance or success. These findings reaffirm how important it is for the teacher to establish a positive emotional climate in the classroom.

Activity 4.1 - Positive and Negative Transfer (HBL, pp. 67-71)

Transfer is the most powerful principle of learning. It is usually provoked by an environmental event. For students, the teacher can be the event that triggers transfer and dumps past experiences (including emotion-laden ones) into the working memory.

A. Write here a brief example of how you use positive transfer in your class or school.

_____

_____

_____

_____

_____

B. Write here a brief example of how negative transfer could occur in your class or school.

_____

_____

_____

_____

_____

C. Discuss A and B above with a partner.

Activity 4.2 - Similarity (HBL, pp. 72-73 and 79)

When two concepts are **too** similar, the brain is often unable to distinguish one from the other. Examples such as **latitude** and **longitude**; **mitosis** and **meiosis**; and even **their**, **there**, and **they're** can cause problems.

A. Think about and list two or more concepts that are so similar they could cause confusion.

_____

_____

_____

_____

_____

B. How could you present them to minimize confusion?

_____

_____

_____

_____

_____

_____

_____

Activity 4.3 - Unique and Unvarying Elements/Critical Attributes (HBL, pp. 73-74 and 80-81)

A. After reading pages 73-74 and 80-81 (*HBL*), work with a partner to complete the worksheet on the next page, *Identifying Unique and Unvarying Elements*. Try using the analogy map graphic organizers on page 107 of *HBL* to help you decide on the differences between two similar concepts.

Analogy Map

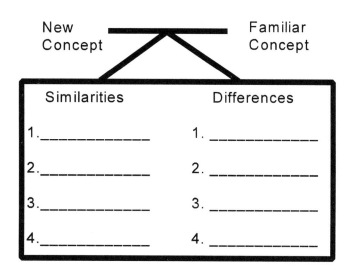

B. After completing the worksheet, decide what benefits identifying the unique and unvarying elements/critical attributes provides to the learner.

_____

_____

_____

C. List here some concepts in your curriculum that would be good candidates for this strategy.

_____

_____

_____

Activity 4.3 Continued

Identifying Unique and Unvarying Elements

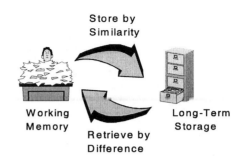

Store by Similarity

Working Memory

Retrieve by Difference

Long-Term Storage

Identify a major concept that you teach and decide on its unique and unvarying elements (critical attributes).

Concept:_____

1. Its unique and unvarying elements (critical attributes) are

_____

_____

2. Simple examples are

_____

_____

3. Complex examples are

_____

_____

4. Student examples are

_____

_____

5. Limits of the unique and unvarying elements (if any) are

_____

Activity 4.4 - Bridging: Transfer of Past to Present (HBL, p. 82)

Directions: After reading page 82 (*HBL*), work with a partner to complete the worksheet below.

The Brooklyn Bridge

BRIDGING

Bridging: Invoking transfer by connecting what the learner knows to other new learning and contexts. Select a concept and use the strategies below to link that concept to the learner's past knowledge.

Brainstorming (applying new learning in other situations):

Look at pages 106-107 (*HBL*) for a graphic organizer that would help with this task.

_____

_____

_____

Analogies (examining similarities and differences):

The Analogy Map could help here.

_____

_____

_____

Metacognition (solving problems by investigating advantages and disadvantages of alternative solutions):

Advantages	Disadvantages

Activity 4.5 - Hugging: Transfer of Present to Future (HBL, p. 83)

Directions: After reading page 83 (*HBL*), work with your partner(s) to complete the worksheet below.

HUGGING

Hugging: Invoking transfer by making the new learning situation more like future situations to which transfer is desired. Select a concept (or the same from Bridging above) and use the strategies below to show how the concept can be useful in future circumstances.

Simulation games (practicing new roles in diverse situations):

_____

_____

_____

_____

Be prepared to present the simulation to the class.

Mental practice (devising mental strategies for dealing with different scenarios):

_____

_____

_____

_____

Contingency learning (secondary learnings needed to accomplish primary learning):

_____

_____

_____

Activity 4.6 - Metaphors (HBL, p. 84)

We used metaphors in designing the Brain Processing Model (Chapter 2 in *HBL* and in Activity 2.1 in this manual) to help remember the important stages in the process.

Directions: Working with a partner, select a concept and decide what metaphor(s) would help you or your students remember it.

Concept:_____

Metaphor(s):

_____

_____

_____

_____

_____

_____

_____

_____

_____

_____

_____

_____

Using Journal Writing to Enhance Transfer and Retention

Journal writing can be a very effective strategy to enhance positive transfer and increase retention. It can be done in nearly all grade levels and subject areas and is particularly effective when used as a closure activity.

Teachers may be reluctant to use this technique because they believe it takes up too much class time while adding more papers for them to evaluate. However, this strategy takes just 3 to 5 minutes, 2 or 3 times a week. The teacher only spot checks journals periodically. The gain in student understanding and retention will be well worth the small amount of time invested.

Here are some suggestions for using journal writing for maximum effectiveness:

- Students should keep a different journal for each class or subject area.

- When used as a closure activity, ask students to write down their responses to these three questions:

  What did we learn today about (insert the *specific* learning objective)?

  How does this connect or relate to what we already know about (insert some past learning that will help students with positive transfer)?

  How can this help us, or how can we use this information/skill in the future?

  Note that these questions are designed to help students find sense and meaning, and to facilitate chunking by making connections to past learning.

- You can use one day's journal entry as a prefocus activity for the following day, provided the new day's lesson is related.

Chapter 5 - Left/Right Brain Processing

Key Points to Ponder

Jot down on this page key points, ideas, strategies, and resources you want to consider later. This sheet is your personal journal summary and will help to jog your memory.

Research Update

Controversy Continues Over Hemispheric Dominance

Perhaps no single piece of brain research has received so much attention and controversy as the notion that the two hemispheres of the brain process information differently. This hemisphere specialization has been demonstrated in numerous research projects since the work of Roger Sperry and his split-brain patients.

Studies on hemispheric specialization led to the notion of hemispheric dominance (or preference). It suggests that when faced with a difficult task, many people are likely to approach the task with a perspective that can be related more closely to one hemisphere's specialization. This is similar, but unrelated, to the notion of handedness. People use either hand to perform a simple task but shift to their dominant hand for a difficult task. Related studies have shown that more males tend to be right-hemisphere dominant, whereas more females tend to be left-hemisphere dominant. This research does have implications for what happens in schools (see *HBL*, pp. 91-96).

Unfortunately, some people have misused this research, referring to themselves, or worse, to students as "too left-brained" or "too right-brained." What is important to remember, however, is that the two hemispheres work together as an integrated *whole*, sharing their different stimuli through the corpus callosum.

Hemispheric dominance is only one component of learning style. Teachers should certainly know about it. But just as a person will catch more footballs using *both* hands, students will learn more when teachers plan a "whole-brain" approach to their lessons.

Is Language Just a Left-Hemisphere Function? (HBL, pp. 86-88)

Dr. Michael Gazzaniga, now at Dartmouth College, continues to work with split-brain patients. In 1996, he reported that the results of working with one patient may indicate that spoken and written language may not reside together in the left hemisphere as previously thought. Spoken language remains primarily a left-hemisphere operation. But this patient revealed that writing was, for her, a right-hemisphere function. Gazzaniga noted that reading and writing arose in our culture long after the speech centers -- which enhanced our survival -- were established. He speculated it is possible that the brain established the reading and writing areas wherever there was spare room. More testing will follow.

Activity 5.1 - Left/Right Brain Functions (HBL, pp. 85-88)

A. Summarize on the diagram below the apparent functions of the left and right hemispheres. Then share your responses with your partner(s).

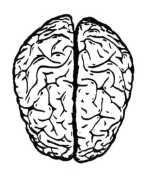

LEFT SIDE   RIGHT SIDE

_____   _____
_____   _____
_____   _____
_____   _____
_____   _____
_____   _____
_____   _____
_____   _____
_____   _____

B. How does what you have written above compare with your previous notions about how the human brain processes information?

_____

_____

_____

Activity 5.2 - Assessing Your Left/Right Dominance (HBL, pp. 89-90)

Take the instrument on pages 89-90 (*HBL*) to assess your own left/right hemispheric dominance and determine your score.

CIRCLE YOUR SCORE BELOW

1--2--3--4--5--6--7--8--9--10--11--12--13--14--15--16--17--18--19--20--21

Left Dominance　　　　　　　**Balanced**　　　　　　　**Right Dominance**

A. Did your score surprise you? Why or why not?

_____

_____

_____

B. Describe here what your score may tell you about your teaching.

_____

_____

_____

_____

C. What implications does what you wrote in B above have for your students?

_____

_____

_____

_____

D. Discuss your responses to A through C above with a partner.

Activity 5.3 - Hemisphericity and Modality Preferences (HBL, p. 90)

Use the chart below to decide what types of classroom strategies would work best with students whose hemisphere and modality preferences (see Activity 2.5) are as indicated. Use the **bridging** and **hugging** strategies you learned in **Chapter 4** to help you with this.

Modality	Left Hemisphere Preference	Right Hemisphere Preference
Visually Preferred		
Kinesthetically Preferred		
Auditorily Preferred		

Activity 5.3 Continued

A. What were your hemispheric and modality preferences?

Hemispheric Preference:_____

Modality Preference(s):_____

B. How did *your* preferences above influence the strategies you designed in the chart for Activity 5.3? Jot down the results of your analysis here.

_____

_____

_____

_____

_____

_____

_____

_____

_____

_____

_____

C. Discuss your analysis with a partner.

Activity 5.4 - Imagery (HBL, p. 103)

Directions: With a partner select an event (such as a shopping or vacation trip, wedding, etc.) and describe it below *using imagery strategies*. Be prepared to share your story with the class.

_____

_____

_____

_____

_____

_____

_____

_____

_____

_____

_____

_____

_____

_____

_____

Activity 5.4 Continued

Directions: With a partner, outline below a short lesson that uses imagery strategies.

_____

_____

_____

_____

_____

_____

_____

_____

_____

_____

_____

_____

_____

_____

_____

Activity 5.5 - Graphic Organizers (HBL, pp. 105-107)

Directions: In groups of three, select an *event* (such as a trip, wedding, finding a new home, selecting a college, etc.) and use a graphic organizer pictured on pages 105-107 (*HBL*), or design your own if you prefer. Use the space below for planning, and so forth. Then draw the organizer on chart paper and present it to the class.

Activity 5.5 Continued

Directions: Still in groups of three, select a curriculum concept and select (or design) a graphic organizer. Draw it below and fill it in.

Chapter 6 - Thinking Skills and Learning

Key Points to Ponder

Jot down on this page key points, ideas, strategies, and resources you want to consider later. This sheet is your personal journal summary and will help to jog your memory.

_____

_____

_____

_____

_____

_____

_____

_____

_____

_____

_____

_____

Research Update

Higher-Order Thinking Increases Understanding and Retention

Although the number of neurons in our brains declines as we age, our ability to learn, remember, and recall is dependent largely on the *number of connections* between neurons. The stability and permanency of these connections depend on the nature of the thinking process and the type and degree of rehearsal that occurred during the learning episode.

PET scans show that elaborative rehearsal, involving higher-order thinking skills, engages the brain's frontal lobe. This engagement helps learners make connections between past and new learning, creates new pathways, strengthens existing pathways, and increases the likelihood that the new learning will be consolidated and stored for future retrieval.

Many teachers recognize the need to do more activities that require elaborate thinking rather than just rote rehearsal. They admit that when they move up through higher levels of Bloom's Taxonomy (or any other thinking skills framework) students demonstrate a much greater depth of understanding. However, they also admit that there are barriers to using this approach regularly because it takes more time. Examples of the barriers they cite are the pressures to cover an ever-expanding curriculum and the tyranny of quick-answer testing of all types.

These barriers will not be overcome easily, but teachers *can work toward a compromise* — finding ways to engage the novel brain with challenging activities and developing alternative assessment strategies.

Activity 6.1 - The Nature of Thinking (HBL, p. 112)

Read the call-out box and accompanying paragraphs on page 112 (*HBL*). Record below whether you agree or disagree with the statements and discuss them with your partner(s).

_____

_____

_____

Activity 6.2 - Bloom's Taxonomy of the Cognitive Domain (HBL, pp. 114-119)

Directions: With a partner, explain verbally what the pictorial view below is all about. Then fill in the chart on the next page, using the explanation of the pictures to describe your thought processing at each level of the taxonomy.

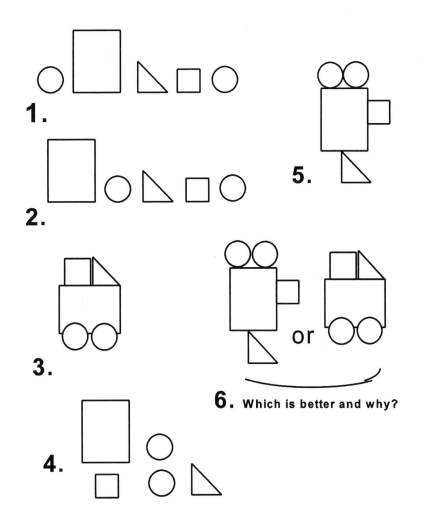

Activity 6.2 Continued

Directions: Write on the lines below the six levels of Bloom's taxonomy, starting with the least complex at the bottom. Then write a few words next to each level that describe the type of processing that occurs when describing the various pictures on the previous page.

LEVEL	DESCRIPTION of PROCESSING
6.	
5.	
4.	
3.	
2.	
1.	

Activity 6.2 Continued

Take a Concept/Situation . . . UP THE TAXONOMY!

Directions: With a partner, think of a task that you need to accomplish with your own child, parent, colleague, spouse, and so on (e.g., how to use the washing machine with different types of clothes, using the microwave oven, planning a vacation) and describe questions or activities that move the task up Bloom's Taxonomy.

CONCEPT/SITUATION:_____

Evaluation (judging material using certain criteria):

_____

_____

Synthesis (putting ideas together to form a new whole):

_____

_____

Analysis (breaking down a concept and looking for relationships):

_____

_____

Application (using a concept or principle in a new situation):

_____

_____

Comprehension (translating the material to achieve understanding):

_____

_____

Knowledge (rote remembering of information):

_____

_____

Activity 6.3 - Difficulty and Complexity (HBL, pp. 121-123)

Directions: After reading pages 121-123 in *HBL*, answer the questions below.

What is meant by complexity of thought?

_____

_____

_____

_____

What is meant by difficulty of thought?

_____

_____

_____

_____

Assessing My Understanding of the Difference Between Complexity and Difficulty:

First, let's try a real-life application.

Directions:

1. Select a partner and decide who is Partner A and who is Partner B.

2. Each partner will perform, **in turn**, the activities for each of the three situations in the table at the top of page 63.

3. When both partners have completed the three situations, discuss whether complexity or difficulty was changed **in each situation** when moving from Partner A's activity to Partner B's activity. Was the complexity/difficulty increased or decreased in each instance?

Activity 6.3 Continued

	Deciding Whether Complexity or Difficulty is Increased		
Situation	Partner A's Activity	Partner B's Activity	Complexity or Difficulty Changed? How?
1	Tell your partner the month of your birth and the city and state where you were born.	Tell your partner the make of your current automobile.	
2	Roll a piece of paper into a ball. Stand 10 feet from your partner. Ask your partner to stand and to form his/her arms into a ring in front (as though to hug someone). Now toss the ball five times and try to get all five tosses through the ring formed by your partner's arms.	Repeat what your partner just did, **except** stand facing away from your partner and toss the paper ball over your head five times, still aiming for your partner's ringed arms.	
3	Fanfold a piece of paper. Then explain to your partner three uses for the folded paper.	After listening to your partner's explanation of the uses, choose one you think is best and explain why.	

Now, let's try a school situation.

Directions: Examine how each teacher below changes Activity A to Activity B. Then decide if the teacher has increased that activity's level of complexity or difficulty.

	Deciding Whether Complexity or Difficulty is Increased		
Teacher	Activity A	Activity B	Increased Complexity or Difficulty?
1	Make an outline of the story you just read.	Make an outline of the last two stories you read.	
2	Compare and contrast the personalities of Julius Caesar and Macbeth.	After reading three acts of Macbeth, write a plausible ending.	
3	Choose one character in the story you would like to be and explain your choice.	Choose two characters in the story you would like to be and explain why.	
4	Name the three most common chemical elements on Earth.	Describe in your own words what is meant by a chemical element.	

Activity 6.3 Continued

Is complexity or difficulty more closely related to intelligence?

_____

_____

How will that affect my teaching?

_____

_____

_____

Summary: Increasing the *difficulty* of a task adds to the students' efforts without increasing the level of their thinking processes. Think of it as moving *horizontally* within a level of Bloom's Taxonomy. Strategies such as repetition and drill tend to increase difficulty. Jot down below some other strategies that increase difficulty.

_____

_____

_____

Increasing the *complexity* of a task causes the students to change the way they mentally process the task. Think of it as moving *vertically* up Bloom's Taxonomy from one level to a higher one. Strategies that cause students to compare *and* contrast, or to choose among options and defend their choice, are examples of increasing complexity. Jot down below some other strategies that increase complexity.

_____

_____

_____

_____

Chapter 7 - Putting It All Together

Key Points to Ponder

Jot down on this page key points, ideas, strategies, and resources you want to consider later. This sheet is your personal journal summary and will help to jog your memory.

Research Update

There is still no "one-strategy-fits-all."

The more we learn about the brain, the more we realize how splendidly unique each one is. Thus, no strategy will work all the time with all learners. The key to successful teaching is not only having an ever-increasing repertoire of research-based strategies but knowing when to select the one most likely to result in learning in *that situation*. This conditional knowledge — knowing *when* to use a specific strategy — is, in my opinion, the unique talent of a truly masterful teacher.

Activity 7.1 - Lesson Design (HBL, pp. 130-131)

A. Discuss with your partner(s) the nine components of daily lesson design. Jot down here any questions, concerns, or insights from the discussion that should be shared with the entire group.

_____

_____

_____

B. Here's a sample lesson design using the information processing model in Chapter 2 (*HBL*, page 11). Discuss other ways that the parts below could be changed while still achieving the same objective.

Objective: The learner will be able to describe verbally the major parts of the brain processing model in the text *How the Brain Learns*.

Anticipatory Set: Take a moment to think about whether it is important for teachers to know how we believe the brain selects and processes information. Then discuss your thoughts with your partner.

Purpose: The purpose of this lesson is to give you some of the latest research we have on how we think the brain processes information so that you can be more successful in choosing those teacher actions that are more likely to result in learning.

Input: Describe major steps in the process, including uptake by senses, interplay of the perceptual register and short-term memory, working memory, long-term storage, the cognitive belief system, and self-concept. Emphasize the importance of sense and meaning, and of past experiences in the entire process.

Modeling: Explain why you chose the four metaphors (venetian blinds, clipboard, work table, and filing cabinets). Use examples of working memory capacity, use hands as model, and show the rubber brain.

Check for Understanding: Have students fill in the function sheet after several parts of the model are covered, and have them use the synergy strategy to discuss with their partners.

Guided Practice: Give examples of sense and meaning differences and of positive and negative self-concept differences to determine the extent of application of the model.

Closure: Take a few minutes to quietly summarize in your mind the major parts of the brain processing model, and be prepared to explain them.

Independent Practice: Visit teachers' classrooms to determine the extent to which they use the model in presenting their lessons.

Activity 7.2 - Putting It All Together!

Directions: Working in groups of three, your task is to select two to three particularly important items that you have learned in this course and present them to the class in a *creative* manner, following the guidelines below.

Guidelines:

1. The presentation is limited to *10 minutes or less*.

2. *All* members of the group must participate in the presentation, together or individually.

3. The presentation should reflect appropriate use of some of the brain-based strategies you learned.

4. Be sure that you include activities involving the three major modalities (visual, auditory, and kinesthetic) for the audience.

Selected Bibliography

The titles here are in *addition* to those listed in the *HBL* bibliography. They include additional resource materials as well as interesting articles and texts that have appeared since the publication of *How the Brain Learns*.

Armstrong, T. (1994). *Multiple intelligences in the classroom*. Alexandria, VA: Association for Supervision and Curriculum Development.

Begley, S. (1996, Feb. 19). Your child's brain. *Newsweek*, 55-62.

Bower, G. H. (1992). How might emotions affect learning? In S. A. Christianson (Ed.), *The handbook of emotion and memory: Research and theory* (pp. 3-31). Hillsdale, NJ: Erlbaum.

Caine, R., & Caine, G. (1997). *Educating on the edge of possibility*. Alexandria, VA: Association for Supervision and Curriculum Development.

Elias, M., Zins, J. E., Weissberg, R. P., Frey, K. S., Greenberg, M. T., Haynes, N. M., Kessler, R., Schwab-Stone, M. E., & Schriver, T. P. (1997). *Promoting social and emotional learning*. Alexandria, VA: Association for Supervision and Curriculum Development.

Goleman, D. (1995). *Emotional intelligence*. New York: Bantam Books.

Healy, J. (1990). *Endangered minds: Why our children don't think*. New York: Touchstone.

Hyerle, D. (1996). *Visual tools for constructing knowledge*. Alexandria, VA: Association for Supervision and Curriculum Development.

Jensen, E. (1995). *The learning brain*. Del Mar, CA: Turning Point.

Redenbach, S. (1996). *Autobiography of a dropout: Dear diary*. Davis, CA: Esteem Seminar.

Schacter, D. (1996). *Searching for memory: The brain, the mind, and the past*. New York: Basic Books.

Sousa, D. (1995). *How the brain learns*. Reston, VA: National Association of Secondary School Principals.

Sylvester, R. (1995). *A celebration of neurons: An educator's guide to the human brain*. Alexandria, VA: Association for Supervision and Curriculum Development.

Some Internet Sites:

Whole Brain Atlas. Anatomy of the brain: http://www.med.harvard.edu/AANLIB/

Medical journals for research articles: http://www.ama-assn.org/med_link/peer.htm

Columbia Healthcare. Animated information on body systems: http://www.columbia.net

National Institute of Health. Lots of good information: http://www.nih.gov

Masters for Copying

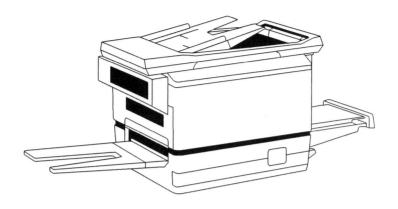

The following pages contain black line masters that can be copied and used along with the material in *How the Brain Learns* and in this *Manual*. Permission for copying is limited to these pages only and is granted on condition that the copies

- ▸ Are not sold

- ▸ Are limited to classroom and staff development use only

- ▸ Have the copyright source clearly printed on all copies

All other copyright restrictions listed at the front of *How the Brain Learns* and the *Manual* remain in effect.

Brain Processing Model

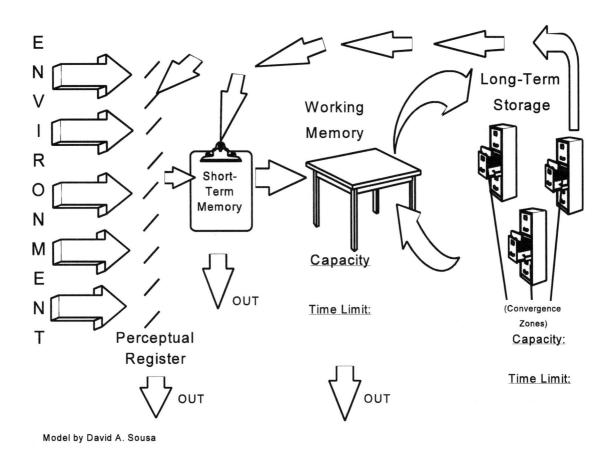

E
N
V
I
R
O
N
M
E
N
T

Short-
Term
Memory

OUT

Perceptual
Register

OUT

Working
Memory

Capacity

Time Limit:

OUT

Long-Term
Storage

(Convergence
Zones)

Capacity:

Time Limit:

Model by David A. Sousa

*Learning Manual for **How the Brain Learns.*** Copyright © 1998 by David A. Sousa.
Photocopying permissible for classroom and staff development use only.

The Brooklyn Bridge

BRIDGING

Bridging: Invoking transfer by connecting what the learner knows to other new learning and contexts.

Brainstorming (applying new learning in other situations):

_____

_____

_____

_____

Analogies (examining similarities and differences):

_____

_____

_____

_____

Metacognition (solving problems by investigating advantages and disadvantages of alternative solutions):

Advantages	Disadvantages

*Learning Manual for **How the Brain Learns.** Copyright © 1998 by David A. Sousa.
Photocopying permissible for classroom and staff development use only.

HUGGING

Hugging: Invoking transfer by making the new learning situation more like future situations to which transfer is desired.

Simulation games (practicing new roles in diverse situations):

_____

_____

_____

_____

_____

Mental practice (devising mental strategies for dealing with different scenarios):

_____

_____

_____

_____

_____

Contingency learning (secondary learnings needed to accomplish primary learning):

_____

_____

_____

_____

_____

Learning Manual for **How the Brain Learns.** Copyright © 1998 by David A. Sousa.
Photocopying permissible for classroom and staff development use only.

Identifying Unique and Unvarying Elements

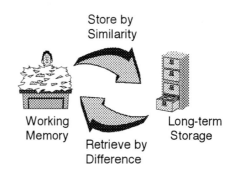

Store by Similarity

Working Memory

Long-term Storage

Retrieve by Difference

Identify a major concept that you teach and identify its unique and unvarying elements (critical attributes).

Concept:_____

1. Its unique and unvarying elements (critical attributes) are

_____

_____

2. Simple examples are

_____

_____

3. Complex examples are

_____

_____

4. Student examples are

_____

_____

5. Limits of the unique and unvarying elements (if any) are

_____

Learning Manual for How the Brain Learns. Copyright © 1998 by David A. Sousa.
Photocopying permissible for classroom and staff development use only.

Take a Concept/Situation . . . UP THE TAXONOMY!

Directions: Think of a concept in your area and design questions or activities that move it up Bloom's Taxonomy.

CONCEPT/SITUATION:_____

Evaluation (judging material using certain criteria):

_____

_____

Synthesis (putting ideas together to form a new whole):

_____

_____

Analysis (breaking down a concept and looking for relationships):

_____

_____

Application (using a concept or principle in a new situation):

_____

_____

Comprehension (translating the material to achieve understanding):

_____

_____

Knowledge (rote remembering of information):

_____

_____

*Learning Manual for **How the Brain Learns.*** Copyright © 1998 by David A. Sousa.
Photocopying permissible for classroom and staff development use only.

To order more copies of this book, fill out the form below!

ORDER FORM

D8312

(For faster service, photocopy this form and send with your P.O.)

CORWIN PRESS, INC.
A Sage Publications Company
2455 Teller Road
Thousand Oaks, CA 91320-2218
Federal ID Number 77-0260369

(Professional books may be tax-deductible.)

Call: 805-499-9774 or
Fax: 805-499-0871 or
E-mail: order@corwinpress.com
http://www.corwinpress.com

Ship to

Name_____

Title_____

Institution _____

Address _____

City _____ State _____ ZIP + 4 _____

Telephone (*Required* for bill-me orders) (_____) _____

Bill to (if different) _____ **P.O.** _____

Institution _____

Attn. _____

Address _____

City _____ State _____ ZIP + 4 _____

Method of Payment

❑ Check enclosed # _____   ❑ VISA   ❑ MasterCard   ❑ DISCOVER

_____

Account Number   Exp. Date

_____

Signature

❑ Please send me your latest free catalog.

❑ Please send me information on _____

Qty.	Title	Book No.	Unit Price	Amount
	Package (Manual & Book)	**82912**	**$39.95**	
	Learning Manual for *How the Brain Learns*	**82852**	**$32.95**	
	Instructor's Guide: Learning Manual for *How the Brain Learns*	**82910**	***$7.50**	

* Instructor's Guide is free with purchase of 10 or more manuals or packages.

** Shipping and handling charges are $3.50 for the first book and $1.00 for each additional book. These charges apply to all orders, including purchase orders and those prepaid by check or credit card. All orders are shipped Ground Parcel unless otherwise requested. Discounts are available for quantity orders — call Customer Service. Prices subject to change without notice. **In Canada, please add 7% GST (12978 6448 RT) and remit in U.S. dollars.** Thank you.

Total Book Order	
In IL, add 6¼% Sales Tax	
In MA, add 5% Sales Tax	
In CA and NY, add appropriate Sales Tax	
In Canada, add 7% GST**	
Subtotal	
Handling Charges**	
Amount Due	

CORWIN
PRESS

The Corwin Press logo — a raven striding across an open book — represents the happy union of courage and learning. We are a professional-level publisher of books and journals for K–12 educators, and we are committed to creating and providing resources that embody these qualities. Corwin's motto is "Success for All Learners."